Ancient Greece

Ancient Greece

and the Mediterranean

Michael Kerrigan

This book is published by
BBC Worldwide Ltd,
Woodlands, 80 Wood Lane,
London W12 0TT

First published in 2001

ISBN 0 563 53760 4

Produced for BBC Worldwide by
Toucan Books Ltd, London

Cover photograph: Robert
Harding Picture Library

Printed and bound in France by
Imprimerie Pollina s.a.
n° L80762-A

Colour separations by
Imprimerie Pollina s.a.

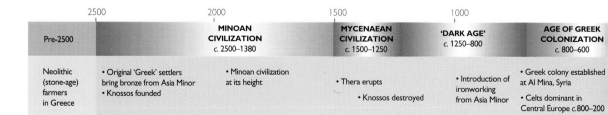

2500		2000		1500		1000	
Pre-2500		**MINOAN CIVILIZATION** *c. 2500–1380*		**MYCENAEAN CIVILIZATION** *c. 1500–1250*		**'DARK AGE'** *c. 1250–800*	**AGE OF GREEK COLONIZATION** *c. 800–600*
Neolithic (stone-age) farmers in Greece	• Original 'Greek' settlers bring bronze from Asia Minor • Knossos founded	• Minoan civilization at its height		• Thera erupts • Knossos destroyed		• Introduction of ironworking from Asia Minor	• Greek colony established at Al Mina, Syria • Celts dominant in Central Europe c.800–200

Contents

500	400	300
PEISISTRATID TYRANNY 545–510	**GOLDEN AGE OF PERICLES** 449–431 **PELOPONNESIAN WAR** 431–404	

• **Solon**'s reforms start democratizing Athens

• First (**Darius**'s) Persian invasion

• Second (**Xerxes**'s) Persian invasion

• **Cleisthenes**'s reforms establish Athenian democracy

• Roman Republic founded

• **Philip II** seizes power in Macedon

• Birth of **Alexander**

• **Philip** dies; **Alexander** becomes King of Macedon

• Death of **Alexander**

AEGEAN ORIGINS

AEGEAN ORIGINS

We revere the Greeks as the founders of Western civilization. Yet 5000 years ago, though other cultures flourished, there was no hint in Greece of the glorious destiny that lay in store. While the pyramids of the pharaohs rose steadily skywards and cities boomed throughout the Near East, the inhabitants of this rugged peninsula scratched a living from their grudging soil. Nor was there anything especially 'Western' about their development when it finally arrived: it was trade with the south and east that encouraged the growth of Greek civilization. Relatively undeveloped though their culture may have been, the Greeks had the crucial virtue of open-mindedness, eagerly embracing the ideas and attitudes of the outside world. It was their easy readiness to be influenced by others which, paradoxically, allowed them to build such a strong identity of their own – one which would carry the fame of Greece to the whole world.

Previous page: Speed, grace, colour and a delight in nature sum up the exuberant spirit of the Minoan civilization in the famous 'Dolphin Fresco' from the New Palace at Knossos, Crete, c.1450 BC.

THE SEA AT THE CENTRE OF THE WORLD

Mountainous, rocky and wild, its scraggy pastures seared by the sun, the land of Greece was not an obvious site for civilization. And for a long time it slumbered unregarded while elsewhere great cities sprang up out of fertile flood plains. Civilizations were growing up along the banks of the Nile and of the Tigris and Euphrates, their wealth underwritten by the bounty of these great rivers. By 2500 BC, Egypt's Old Kingdom was at its height, while farther east in Mesopotamia the Sumerian state was thriving. Through succeeding generations, as one dynasty after another took power, these cultures had their ups and downs – even their disasters. Yet the regions as a whole never looked back; there was so far no indication, however, that Greece had even started to look forward.

The agricultural plenty on which the other civilizations were based was almost completely lacking in Greece, while communication was nothing less than a nightmare in such rough country. Left to its own devices, Greece was unlikely to have made any significant progress. Fortunately, however, it did not have to rely exclusively on its own resources, for around it was the Mediterranean – and in particular, to the east, the sheltered Aegean Sea.

The Aegean is enclosed from three directions, with Greece and the Balkans shielding it to the west and north, and modern Turkey marking out its eastern shore. Along its southern edge is a fringe of islands, not only the tiny Cyclades, but also the larger masses of Crete, Karpathos and Rhodes. These ensure that even on this side the worst storms of the open sea are kept at a distance. With such a convenient maritime highway on Greece's

1. An inhospitable coast, but a blue sea opening out onto the world: the island of Rhodes was a gateway to civilization.

THE ANCIENT AEGEAN

THRACE

Sea of Marmara

Pellas•

Mt Olympus▲

Bosphorus

•Troy

Lesbos

•Pergamon

Euboea

ASIA MINOR

Thermopylae •

Aegean Sea

•Delphi

•Chalcis

Chios

•Sardis

Gulf of Corinth

•Thebes

LYDIA

ATTICA

•Marathon

Corinth •

Salamis

•Athens

Samos

•Ephesus

Mycenae •

•Laurion

Olympia •

Aegina

Argos•

Epidaurus

Delos

IONIA

PELOPONNESE

Cyclades

•Halicarnassus

•Sparta

•Rhodes

Thera

Sea of Crete

Rhodes

Karpathos

Knossos•

Crete

doorstep, difficulties in internal communications mattered much less; nor was the comparative poverty of the land so crucial. Seaborne contact with the world outside gave Greece an advantage to offset other handicaps: the Aegean islands could be the stepping stones of civilization.

The first Greeks

The Greeks themselves probably arrived overland in what we now know as Greece, travelling along the narrow coastal strip between the Thracian mountains and the northern Aegean. They are thought to have originated in the mountains of Anatolia, in the north of what is now Turkey. Greece at that time was by no means empty of human inhabitants – traces of occupation have been found dating back to Neanderthal times and beyond – but the first wave of progress, like so many subsequently, seems to have originated outside the country. Dislodged from their Asian homeland by who knows what pressures of overpopulation or political turmoil, the settlers seem to have edged their way westward around 4500 years ago.

With them they brought bronze, and the knowledge and skills required to work it. The metal had long since been taken for granted in Asia and Egypt, but was as yet unheard of in Europe. An alloy of copper and tin, it is hard and strong in use, hugely versatile, yet simply made. To peoples whose practices had for centuries been set in stone, the impact of metalworking can hardly be overstated. Bronze Age technologies not only

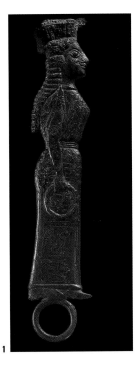

1

1. Imposing yet a little stiff, a bronze mirror-handle from around 600 BC embodies the artistic style of pre-classical Greece.

2. This sumptuous work in gold was fashioned in Anatolia in the 7th century BC – making it one of the first coins ever to be minted.

2

revolutionized work and weaponry, but liberated the imagination, for with adaptability came expressive freedom, an end to the rigid simplicities of stone. For the Greeks, it allowed a new and distinct identity to assert itself through the fashioning of weapons, tools, vessels and utensils, ornaments and jewellery. From the first, that identity would be open-minded and outward-looking, drawing upon influences from throughout the ancient world.

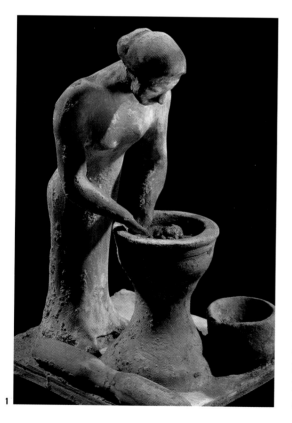

1

MINOAN SPLENDOURS

Typically, the first great flowering of what we now think of as Greek civilization emerged not in Greece itself but on the island of Crete, where in around 2500 BC the palace-complex of Knossos was founded just to the east of Mount Ida near the north coast. It was here that, by about 1900 BC, an astonishing Bronze Age culture had been established. Archaeological investigations in modern times have told us much about the Minoans, while leaving large areas of their life and history still unknown and mysterious.

Named after Minos, the Cretan king who in later Greek myths was held to have ruled over this kingdom, the Minoans were traditionally feared by the peoples of their day for their naval power. Yet when in 1899 the British archaeologist Arthur Evans undertook his first excavations on Crete, he became convinced that he was unearthing a golden civilization founded on plenty, peace and pleasure. The labyrinthine passages at the heart of the vast royal palace of Knossos seem to have been a bursting storehouse of food and drink – testimony, he concluded, to a regime of kingly high-living. No fortifications girded Knossos for war – instead, there were sumptuous wall-paintings and elaborate artefacts that pointed to a 'feminized' culture of artistry and beauty.

Paradoxically, at the heart of this feminine culture lay the bull cult. Carved bull's heads bedecked every building in the palace complex at Knossos, and the image of the bull appears again and again in Minoan pottery, painting and statuary.

In themselves, all these bulls might have suggested a violently masculine symbolism. Yet the athletic forms of the men and women vaulting effortlessly over their charging backs in some of the Minoans' painting and sculpture suggested a brute masculinity transcended by feminine grace and skill. Painted scenes, with flowers and animal figures, testified to the Minoans' love of nature, while figures of bare-breasted women suggested to Evans an unselfconscious sexual freedom which a Victorian Englishman could only dream of.

A harder reality

In recent years, scholars have become more sceptical about Evans's findings. For such a supposedly peaceable people, they point out, the Minoans left an awful lot of weaponry in their shrines and tombs. As for the absence of fortifying walls around their cities – would these really have been needed by an island empire that ruled the waves around? Did the Minoans, they ask, really love nature for itself, or just venerate the deities they happened to associate with natural things? Did the average Minoan woman go bare-breasted as a matter of course? Or was it rather a guise adopted only by priestesses in particular moments of ritual significance?

The discovery in the 1980s of incontrovertible evidence of human sacrifice – and perhaps even ritual cannibalism – has cast the Minoans in a new and more sinister light, though the marvellous sophistication of their civilization can still hardly be doubted.

2

1. This 6th-century BC figurine, just 17 cm (7 in) tall, captures a woman kneading dough.

2. Figures bearing gifts make their way across a 16th-century BC wall-painting in the palace at Knossos.

According to inscriptions at Knossos, the Minoans produced 1.5 kg (3 lb) of wool from every sheep, a yield unsurpassed until modern times.

1

1. Seen here in a sacred
jug, the bull's head was the
central symbol of the
Minoan civilization and
appears everywhere at
Knossos.

2. The flowering of Minoan
athleticism is recorded in
the supreme achievement
of Minoan art: the famous
16th-century BC
bull-leaper's fresco.

2

Women in power?

Evans seems to have been right, to some extent at least, in the most controversial of his views: that of the 'feminine' inclination of Minoan culture. Many experts now believe that, apart from a king who was no more than a figurehead, the key figure at Knossos was a high priestess. The ritual life of this society was thus firmly in the hands of a female-dominated priesthood – though this may not have impinged much upon the everyday lives of women in society at large. The question of whether this was actually a matriarchal society has been a matter of debate in recent years. It is interesting that Minoan sources record no male god of any significance, only the earth goddess Potnia, the 'Lady of the Labyrinth', along with a host of other goddesses who may be no more than manifestations of Potnia's many-faceted power. The one male god, who was both Potnia's consort and her son, seems to have served only to record by his own death and rebirth the passage of the year through dark winter to spring. He would hardly have been needed at all had it not been for the fact that the goddess herself could not be allowed to die. Ultimately, he grew in importance, many centuries later shouldering aside female authority as the great god Zeus: for now, though, he remained a very secondary figure.

1

1. In ancient legend, Knossos was the home of wicked Minos and his Minotaur, seen here being slain by the Greek hero Theseus.

1. The Lion Gate at Mycenae.

2. The power of the bull did not die with Knossos, as this ivory box of the Mycenaean era makes beautifully clear.

attendants, whose fig and wheat rations have been painstakingly noted down. Specialization applied not only to such skills as those of the goldsmith, silversmith, jeweller (one man concerned himself solely in the preparation of 'blue-glass paste'), ivory carver and perfumer, but also to rural trades such as shepherd, goatherd, cowherd, huntsman and woodcutter, as well as to marine occupations such as Pylos's 200-strong coastguard and the 600 rowers in its fleet. Women recorded on the payrolls – in addition to the bath attendants – included corn-grinders, flax-workers and spinners.

So while Mycenae's massive Lion Gate does indeed appear to shout warlike defiance at the world, the truth is probably less straightforward. The monumental architecture and intimidating appearance that were standard for Mycenaean centres were perhaps more a matter of presentation – an assertion of state power. Once inside those imposing walls, the impression we have is not of monolithic mass, but of intricate organization, with workshops and storehouses as systematically arranged as were the activities of the workers that they housed.

Along with all this quiet industry, of course, the Pylos tablets do hint at the Mycenaeans' more aggressive side: not only is an impressive output of military equipment and weaponry documented, but there are records of large numbers of captive slaves. No one, then, could imagine that the Mycenaeans were a people of peace, yet the men Schliemann believed were the sackers of cities do seem to have been driven as much by mercantile as by military considerations.

The Mycenaeans made this exquisite earring.

The wooden horse of Troy steps out on this Mycenaean jar.

THE TRUTH ABOUT TROY

Greek tradition always associated the war of Troy with the Mycenaean age, and for a long time modern scholars were inclined to agree with it, setting the conflict at some time in the 13th century BC. Many are still persuaded by Schliemann's claim to have discovered the actual site of Troy at Hissarlik in the Dardanelles, though there really is no way of being certain about it. Schliemann's insistence that he had found the Greek king Agamemnon's palace at Mycenae is a good deal less convincing. The tombs he uncovered there turn out to date from a pre-Mycenaean age well before his presumed date for the Trojan War. Homer, meanwhile, is a confusing guide: his heroes' boar's-head helmets and high, straight-sided tower shields would have seemed old-fashioned even in Mycenaean times. Their iron-bladed swords and cremation of their dead, on the other hand, would place the conflict in a later age altogether. An increasing number of experts are coming to see the 'war' as just another dark age raid, exaggerated and glorified in the telling. The fact is that we will probably never know the truth about Troy, though the legends are surely at least rooted in historical fact.

DARK ANARCHY

Stepping into the breach left by the decline of Knossos, the Mycenaeans dominated trade in the eastern Mediterranean between 1340 and 1250 BC. Then their power in its turn imploded. Nobody really knows why, though the answer may have lain in the world outside Greece. A state that depended so much on commerce with Asia Minor (the Asian part of modern Turkey) may not have been able to cope when its trading partners in the east were gripped by economic crisis and political turmoil. The disturbances caused large-scale population movements in the eastern Mediterranean: the raids of the mysterious 'Sea Peoples' and the invasion of the nomadic Dorians from the north. Both groups have been blamed for the overthrow of the Mycenaean civilization, but the truth is almost certainly more complicated. Most likely these groups moved in to occupy the vacuum left by a civilization already well into its terminal decline. Little is known of the 'dark age' that followed, a time in which local war-lords jostled for advantage and the advance of civilization appears to have been put on hold.

Of gods and heroes

Yet it was a time, too, when important aspects of the Greek identity began to be established. It was during this period, for example, that a single set of

1

1. Shield waving, Athena emerges from the head of her father Zeus, armed for action on behalf of the Greek peoples.

gods took over the role until now discharged by myriad local deities. At the top of Mount Olympus in northern Greece, thunderbolt-wielding Zeus and his queen Hera were reputed to have their thrones; with them lived Poseidon the earth-shaker, god of the sea, Apollo the sun-god and Ares, god of war. The huntress Artemis, goddess of the moon, was as icily chaste as Aphrodite, goddess of love, was passionate. Zeus's favourite daughter Athena, goddess of industry and artistic endeavour, was said to have sprung fully formed from her father's brow, while Hermes, the wing-footed messenger, carried tidings between the heavens and earth.

The mythology that took shape around this pantheon united communities the length and breadth of Greece. It provided a common frame of reference for people who may have thought they shared little else. Soon, in fact, they would share one more thing: a love of Homer's *Iliad* and *Odyssey*, two great epic poems in which the Olympian gods figured as all too fallibly human characters. At some time in the 8th century BC, Homer, whoever he was (or, for that matter, whoever they were, for some scholars doubt that any one author could have written both poems), fixed in writing legends that had long been handed down by bards in the oral tradition. From that time onwards, the Homeric poems, still among the greatest works of Western literature, would help define what it was to be Greek, as much for the Greeks themselves as for the wider world. Homer's tales of the clangorous battles fought before the gates of Troy, and of the resourceful Odysseus' long and perilous home-coming at war's end together gave Greeks a stirring set of stories with whose heroes they could all identify. The other sense in which the Homeric poems would represent a breakthrough was that they were written, not in Linear A, B, C or whatever, but in a new and universal Greek alphabet that was modelled on Phoenician script.

 THE WAR IN HEAVEN

The Olympian gods were not the first rulers of the universe. Before them, according to Greek mythology, the Titans had been masters of all. There were 12 of them, the sons and daughters of Uranus (heaven) and Gaia (Earth). At their head was Cronos, father of Zeus (portrayed in bronze, right), who would one day seize power for himself in a heavenly coup. Like most myths, the story has symbolic significance as well as being an exciting tale. The Olympians' victory over the Titans can be seen as representing the triumph of a shared Greek culture and consciousness over the local loyalties that had gone before.

1. Odysseus hears the bewitching song of the Sirens in the *Odyssey*.

2. The infernal ferryman Charon picks up another two souls for passage to the underworld.

3. Achilles kills the Amazon Penthesilea, queen of the warrior women.

4. Thetis gets a weapon for her son Achilles from the god Hephaistos.

A revolution in waiting

In retrospect it can be seen that Greece was quietly getting into place the key ingredients of the incredible rise to come – the traditions, the tales and the shared identity. The upheavals of the dark age are easily overestimated, for while the old élites certainly fell and a hotchpotch of invaders and opportunists seized power for themselves, life for the lower orders may in reality have changed comparatively little. Tilling the soil was just as hard and sailing the sea every bit as hazardous, whatever lord was being served.

There were dangers, inevitably: in the absence of any centralizing authority, feuding was endemic at local level, while no community could feel completely safe from raids by seaborne pirates or overland invaders. Yet much of the time life must have been quiet: if civilization had truly collapsed, it is safe to assume that many in Greece scarcely noticed. And though they may have murdered and ransacked in their greed for booty, the raiders brought boons with them as well: it was to the Dorians, for example, that Greece owed the gift of ironworking.

The properties of iron had long been known, and it could be found in abundance everywhere, but without the equipment required to work it, iron might just as well have been gold. Special furnaces had to be developed for successful smelting (much higher temperatures were needed than for the manufacture of bronze), and smiths had to acquire the art of forging the red-hot metal. Once these skills were mastered, however – as they seem to

4

have been during the first few centuries of the 1st millennium BC – iron was poised to bring about another technological revolution. Every bit as adaptable as bronze, but capable of sustaining a harder edge, iron was cheap enough to be used for a far wider range of applications. While copper was freely available, bronze production was limited by the prohibitive costs of tin, a scarce metal that had to be brought from faraway places such as the Iranian plateau – even perhaps from Cornwall. Despite its adaptability, bronze was used only for prestigious weaponry and utensils, while iron was used for humbler tools. Ploughshares, sickles, hammers, nails and blades – weapons not just for the lord, but for the ordinary man.

THE RISE OF
THE GREEKS

THE RISE OF THE GREEKS

As Greece entered the first millennium BC, it looked as though civilization had been and gone. The glories of Mycenae were now no more than a fading memory. Where once a mighty empire had held sway, warlords exacted what tribute they could from an impoverished peasantry. Fragmentation and bickering rivalry were the hallmark of Greek 'civilization' at this time. The instinct to build states and institutions seemed to have disappeared, so preoccupied had the heirs of Mycenae become with the need merely to survive from one raid, one harvest to the next. Beneath the anarchic social surface, however, an ever-strengthening Greek identity was taking shape, giving scattered communities a sense of common purpose, if not necessarily a mutual affection. With hindsight, at least, it can be seen that the dark age was not as unrelievedly black as it has been painted: its 'darkness' was that of the hour before the dawn.

FROM HILLFORT TO CITY-STATE

The people of dark-age Greece lived in countless
tiny, scattered settlements, far removed from any
sense of a grander, overarching state. The under-
lying social contract was simple: the *basileus* (local
warlord) and his men provided protection in return
for labour on the land. Ordinary families lived in
mud-brick hovels clustered around the basileus's
fortified hilltop home, yet even his accommodation
would have been anything but palatial. Although
spared the unremitting toil that was the common
lot in those times, the lord and his warriors hardly
led lives of aristocratic luxury. It was a difficult and
impoverished life for the people, but as long as their
lord remained strong it was a safe one. They need
not fear being snatched away from family and
friends and sold into slavery.

   Warlords enriched themselves by raiding one
another for stock and slaves, which were the main
currency in an economy that had yet to conceive of
money. Such wealth could be hoarded at home or
traded outside for imported luxuries. As time went
on, a hierarchy emerged as certain basilei began to
rise above the majority of their fellows. The dominance of the few would, paradoxically, pave the
way for democracy.

   For as warlords grew in power and prosperity,
they ceased to be simple soldiers and became
consumers, developing more sophisticated tastes
for fine clothes and furnishings, beautifully crafted
weapons and household objects, good food and
wine. Many of these had to be imported from
abroad, which meant that high-quality goods had

1

2

1. The focus of social life in
the dark age was the great
hall of the local warlord:
here, slaves carry food in
for a banquet.

2. Patients line up to see
the doctor. The symbolic
serpent of Asclepius, god of
medicine, looks on from a
nearby tree.

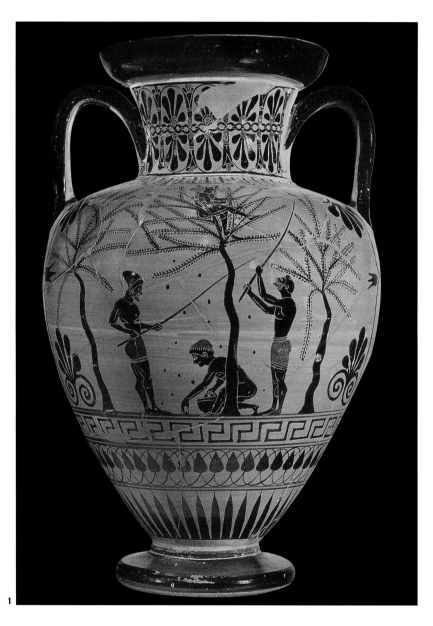

1

1. Whatever the wars and feuding, the rhythms of agricultural life went on: peasants gather olives in this painting from a 6th-century BC vase.

2. One priest pours wine into the flames as another holds out meat for roasting in a sacrificial scene from a 5th-century BC vase.

to be made in Greece in order to be exchanged on the overseas market. A new 'middle class' of freemen – merchants, craftsmen, larger-scale farmers – arose to serve this new demand, a group which would come to rival the aristocracy in economic power. Around the opulent strongholds of the wealthiest basilei, small cities were taking form, in which the warlord's wants increasingly

had to be balanced with those of his citizens. In their physical form these settlements were like larger-scale versions of the hamlets of old: the lord up on his fortified *acropolis* (citadel), the housing of the people huddled below. Beyond lay the fields and olive groves, still the community's economic engine and very much a part of the city, for the ancient Greeks never saw town and country as

2

separate in the way we do. The agora at the city's heart was a new development, however: an open space specially designated for the citizens to walk and talk. That men's opinions, freely expressed, might actually matter in the scheme of things was a conception new to Greece, and as far as we know without precedent in any other civilization. The polis, or city-state, was the great political invention of ancient Greece – and was, indeed, the origin of the modern word 'politics'. For the moment, at any rate, the aristocracy still exercised unquestioned power, but the very existence of the agora hinted at the way things might be changing.

Iron Age equivalents

Not all of these trends were unique to Greece. To the northwest, in central Europe, a parallel tendency can be seen in the emergent culture of the Celts. Flourishing between 1800 to 450 BC, what is known as the Hallstatt culture, after the Austrian salt mines that helped underwrite its wealth, showed a comparable concentration of economic and political power in a few great warlords.

Their taste for luxury goods – testified to by the sumptuous splendour in which many chiefs were buried – likewise created a caste of comparatively affluent craftsmen and merchants buoyed up economically by a thriving export and import market. A sword recovered from one Hallstatt grave testifies not only to consummate craftsmanship, but also to the extensive trading network of which Celtic society was the centre: its handle of oriental ivory is exquisitely inlaid with Baltic amber. Ceramics, fine metalwork and glass, as well as the wine the Celts notoriously loved: all these were imported from the Mediterranean in return for weapons and luxuries of Celtic manufacture. Similar settlements from what are now Poland and Slovenia in the east to France and Britain in the west eventually grew, like their counterparts in Greece, into small-scale cities.

 THE MARRIAGE AT MARSEILLES

The tale is told of how the Greek colony at Massilia (now Marseilles) was established around 600 BC. Landing on the Gallic shore to trade, Euxenes of Phocis was invited to a feast by Namos, king of the native Segobrigai. The king's daughter Petta fell in love with the visitor and presented him with a bowl of wine mixed with water as a sign that she had chosen him in marriage. Her father approved her choice, and the dynasty they founded led Massilia for several centuries.

A TEMPLATE FOR CIVILIZATION

Commerce was so vital to the Greeks' developing economy that, between 800 and 600 BC, many of them moved abroad, setting up cities in trading territories overseas. In this way they could assure an uninterrupted two-way traffic. Along with this, perhaps, was the increasing aspiration of a class of energetic young men who, if they could not belong to the ranks of the rulers at home, were determined to find a way of doing so abroad. Following the same pattern they had come to know – streets of mud-brick houses around an open agora beneath an elevated acropolis fortified in stone – these colonies

were Greek homes away from home. And they were no mere trading posts, but sizeable cities: the colony at Pithekoussai, in southern Italy, seems to have had a population of several thousand. From the Black Sea, North Africa and Italy to the coasts of France and Spain, such colonies brought the known world into commercial and cultural contact with Greece. The consequences for both sides were far-reaching.

1. Now associated with the Atlantic fringes of Europe, the Celts were once the continent's central military and economic power.

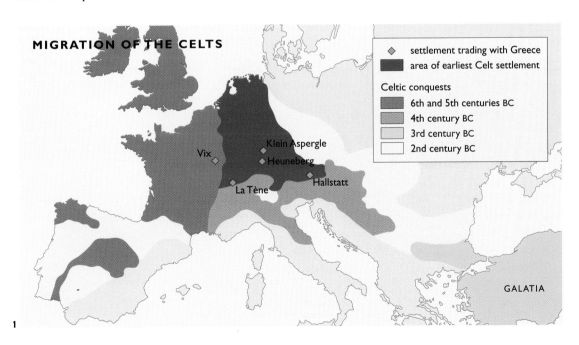

MIGRATION OF THE CELTS

◇ settlement trading with Greece
■ area of earliest Celt settlement

Celtic conquests
6th and 5th centuries BC
4th century BC
3rd century BC
2nd century BC

Vix
Klein Aspergle
Heuneberg
Hallstatt
La Tène

GALATIA

1

1. A 4th-century BC family offers up a ram in supplication to Dionysus.

1

Many of the earliest colonies were sited just a short hop away across the Aegean, as at Ephesus and Miletus on Asia Minor's western coast. As time went on, however, more far-flung settlements were established around the northern shores of Turkey, across the Black Sea at Tanais in what is now the Ukraine, and in Cheronesus in the modern Crimea. From Greece's western coast, meanwhile, adventurers set forth over the Adriatic to establish cities in southern Italy and Sicily. Naples and Syracuse were both originally Greek trading colonies, as was Massilia (now Marseilles) in southern France. From this base at the mouth of the Rhone, Greek merchants could not only trade with the peoples of southern France, but also reach upriver to the Celtic heartlands of Central Europe. Though in some cases native populations were driven out to make way for the Greek colonizers, overall local people appear to have been net gainers – otherwise, the settlers would scarcely have been able to survive in such isolation so far from home.

The Greeks took the local people's agricultural surpluses off their hands, as well as locally produced raw materials, in return for fine pottery and luxury goods of all kinds. The wealth of relics that have been unearthed by modern researchers at such sites makes abundantly clear the eagerness with which local populations took to these Greek imports, and Greek manufacturers were influenced in their turn. A geometric pattern, a floral motif, an unfamiliarly shaped bowl or vase: archaeological finds both from the colonies themselves and from their mother cities in mainland Greece reveal that Greek potters and other craftsmen were adapting traditional designs to suit foreign tastes – for profit, of course, but also, no doubt, for their own aesthetic pleasure.

An African polis

At Naucratis in the Nile Delta, one major colony brought Greece to the pharaohs' doorstep. Written evidence and archaeological finds attest to a busy trade that, from around 630 BC onward, passed through the place. Greek merchants brought silver, olive oil and wine, as well as ornate pottery and other manufactured luxuries, in return for papyrus, linen and grain for home consumption. Naucratis was to all intents and purposes a Greek city, with temples to Aphrodite, Hera and Apollo and streets set out on the already traditional grid plan. Only the acropolis was missing, since the mud flats of the Delta did not furnish any natural vantage points. Instead, it seems, a fort was constructed to provide protection against attack.

Any raid was likely to come not from Egypt itself but from opportunistic pirates from the sea, for

 THE MERCHANT ADVENTURERS

The development of Phoenician culture often seems to have paralleled that of the early Greeks. A seafaring people, originally from the coast of what is now southern Lebanon and northern Israel, the Phoenicians established colonies of their own all around the Mediterranean, often settling and trading alongside the Greeks. Phoenician merchants (depicted in this statue, right) brought to the civilizations of the eastern Mediterranean and Near East such raw materials as silver, gold and copper from Spain, Portugal and northwest Africa. They may even have ventured as far as Cornwall to obtain tin. Their breakaway colony of Carthage evolved into an imperial power in its own right, for a time threatening to eclipse the rise of Rome.

relations with the host people seem to have been stable, if not exactly warm. The two sides were brought together by bonds of mutual convenience and advantage, though the partnership proved an enduring one for all that. The Egyptians, according to the Greek historian Herodotus, bitterly resented what they considered their cultural contamination by the Greeks: 'No Egyptian, man or woman', he said, 'will kiss a Greek, or use a Greek knife, spit, or cauldron, or even eat the flesh of a bull known to be clean, if it has been cut by a Greek knife.'

For their part, however, the Greeks could put up with such hostility cheerfully enough, knowing that, however grudging, their hosts could not bear to be without their pottery and other products. This taste for all things Greek is amply confirmed by the archaeological record. Items have turned up at all the major sites relating to this period. Greek architecture, wall-paintings and ceramic designs of the 7th and 6th centuries, meanwhile, all betray the influence of Egypt's heavy, monumental style.

Yet perhaps the most profound consequence of this colonizing phase was the paradoxical one that by setting up shop abroad the Greeks came to see just how Greek they really were. Strangers on foreign shores, they naturally closed ranks with one another. They were brought together not only by a spirit of self-preservation, but also by a shared nostalgia for their native skies, a shared yearning for Greek food, Greek friends and Greek families. The spirit that was born of the colonial experience was reflected in a growing sense of civic identification at home and in the mounting patriotism of the mother city-states back in Greece.

DICTATORS VERSUS DEMOCRATS

If the Greeks of the 7th century BC felt an ever stronger attachment to the *polis* (city-state), they became increasingly disaffected with the aristocrats who ruled over them. Homer's characterization of the basileus as the 'shepherd of his people' had always seemed idealized, perhaps, yet through the long dark age there had simply been nowhere else to look for leadership. Now an increasingly affluent class of merchants, craftsmen and scribes had won economic privileges for themselves. They did not see why they should look up to lords whom in many cases they rivalled in wealth. Often, indeed, the basilei were in their debt: more concerned than ever in these times of social uncertainty to assert the inherent majesty of their rank, many had to borrow heavily from their inferiors in order to keep up aristocratic appearances. Even the poor were less likely to revere their lords now that there were upwardly mobile commoners whose examples they could dream of emulating.

This slow disintegration of the lords' authority was sharply exacerbated in mid century when it became evident that the old system was failing to such an extent that the Greek cities could no longer feed their rising populations. Desperate for funds, many basilei were leaning more and more heavily on their peasant-farmers for tribute, bringing discontentment to boiling point. With aristocratic rule perceived as a shambles, there was an empty space at the top of Greek society: it might be filled by democratic government on the one hand, or the dictatorship of the *tyrannoi* (tyrants) on the other.

The Athenian experiment

In many Greek cities, of course, it was the military strongman who rose to power. Indeed, many of the most economically advanced and culturally forward-looking of the city-states went down this road. One example was Lydia in western Asia Minor, where the tyrant Gyges first seized power, then had his rule retrospectively confirmed by a sacred soothsayer. That combination of cunning and brazen shamelessness was the hallmark of the successful tyrant.

By the middle of the 7th century BC, tyrannies were springing up all over Greece: Kypselos took charge in Corinth in around 655 to be succeeded by Peirandors his son, while in 640 Theagenes appointed himself sole ruler in the city of Megara, lying roughly halfway between Corinth and Athens. Along the Ionian coast in the northeastern Aegean, where the influence of Persia had long been strong, tyranny often seemed the natural mode of government. Absolutism was the norm here and the traditions of the polis were weaker. There was in any case much to recommend dictatorship, where the dictator was strong and intelligent enough to provide effective government. If tyranny flourished, it was because it gave most Greek cities the sort of rule that they wanted.

The city of Athens, however, chose a different path. Set on a rocky outcrop above the Saronic Gulf on Greece's southeastern side, Athens started out as one of the more backward poleis. The state's aristocracy – who were descendants of the old basilei and their armed retainers – hung on

1

1. This water-clock was used to limit the length of Athenian litigants' speeches.

Democratic Athens's fear of tyranny was enshrined in legislation: it decreed that any man who murdered a would-be tyrant was protected by law.

jealously to its inherited power and wielded it oppressively. No less likely setting could have been imagined for the world's first experiment in democracy. In the end, however, a grasping aristocracy made its government unbearable. Even here the road to freedom was paved with abortive reforms and violent coups: Athens, too, saw its share of tyrants down the decades.

Yet the desire for democracy, once aroused, was never quite extinguished. When in the mid-570s BC, the statesman Solon made a bid for popularity by cancelling all debts, he liberated thousands of Athens' poor from what amounted to (and in some cases legally was) a demoralizing life of debt-slavery. He then promptly gave this grateful electorate a vote at the city's assembly. This may have been an act of the purest political cynicism on his part, but that did not for a moment seem to worry the reform's beneficiaries. Within a few years, though, Solon was dead. His reforms died with him, and the city's aristocracy bounced back to resume the reins of power. Their rule was resented, however, even though for the time being it had to be endured. Never more would the old nobility enjoy the instinctive respect of ordinary Athenians. Nor did the people ever fully accept Peisistratos, the tyrant who came after, though he at least was an effective ruler in a way the aristocrats never were. Twice seizing power, and twice resisted, Peisistratos was not secure in his position until 545 BC. He attempted to buy the city's support by means of major public-building projects: he did much for civic pride, but never quenched the thirst for freedom.

 THE CORINTHIAN BOOM

Terms like 'tyrant' and 'democracy' can easily mislead the modern reader. Tyrannic rule was not necessarily oppressive, and might even enjoy a large measure of popular consent. Tyrants could certainly be very good at getting things done – as even the critics of the Athenian tyrant Peisistratos were obliged to concede. Through much of the 6th century BC, while Athens was making its slow and painful journey towards democracy, the tyranny of Corinth (pictured below) seemed to be leading the way forward for the Greeks at large. Energetic traders and colonists, the Corinthians were also great innovators across the whole spectrum of creative arts. Though their achievements would ultimately be overshadowed by those of classical Athens, for many decades it was the Athenians themselves who were left in the shade.

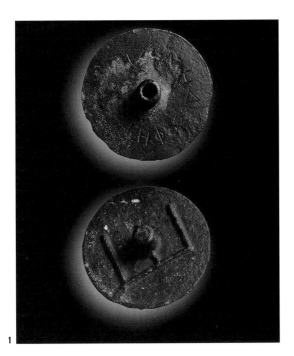

HOW ATHENIAN DEMOCRACY WORKED

ASSEMBLY OF THE PEOPLE
Composed of all Athenian citizens. Divided into ten 'tribes'.

BOULE (COUNCIL)
Composed of 500 men in all – 50 from each of the ten tribes.

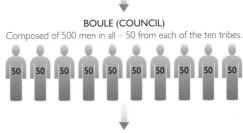

PRYTANEIS (EXECUTIVE COMMITTEE)
The civic year is divided into ten 'months'.
Each tribal group of 50 men from the Boule serves for
one 'month' as the Prytaneis. Each day a new chairman is
selected by ballot.

Chairman

1

2

After Peisistratos's death in 527 BC, his sons
Hippias and Hipparchos took over as rulers, and it
was not until 510 that the Athenians managed to
get back their liberty. Once the tyrants were
expelled from the city, reforms were inaugurated by
Cleisthenes, whose scope was still more radical
than those previously introduced by Solon. Every
freeborn male had the right to participate in the
ekklesia or state assembly, the body that was
entrusted with the task of deciding policy. A
smaller senate conducted the daily business of the
city, though that, too, was elected by all the citizens:
the system of democracy – government by the
demos or people – had finally been established.

1. These little tallies were
placed in an urn by jurors
to indicate their opinion: a
hollow disc meant 'guilty'
and a solid one 'innocent'.

2. Athenian democracy
divided citizens into ten
'tribes' (or electoral
constituencies) for
maximum accountability,
but large swathes of the
population never got to
vote at all.

THE PERSIAN WARS

This remarkable new Athenian order had no sooner been brought into being than it was tested to the very limit by the wars with Persia. Over the decades, this conflict took on some of the aspects of a holy war, so enormous and irreconcilable were the political and cultural differences it represented. On the one hand there was Persia, a vast eastern empire, ruled by autocrats and contemptuous of reform; on the other, there was the city of Athens, first governed, and now defended, by its own free citizenry. No sterner challenge to the Athenians' commitment to liberty could be imagined; while, as for Persia, its ruling caste bitterly despised the autonomy of the poleis in general and Athenian democracy in particular. The emperors seem to have seen Greek citizen-power as a calculated affront to their own highly conservative values.

The shadow falls

Ever since the mid-6th century BC, the might of Persia had cast a darkening shadow over Greece. The poleis looked on in mounting alarm as King Cyrus the Great, the founder of the Persian empire, extended his rule over much of the Near East. The eastern empire soon included the Greek colonies in Asia Minor within its boundaries; by the end of the 6th century the Persian fleet had started picking off Aegean islands.

Greek resentment was tempered to some extent by the commercial opportunities offered by the new relationship with Persia, but by 499 BC the

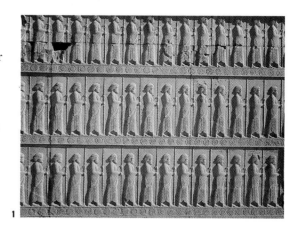

1

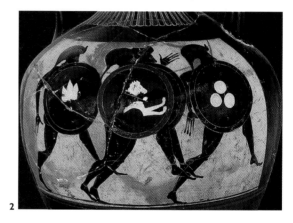

2

1. Armoured imperial soldiers file across this Persian frieze, c.500 BC.

2. Military messengers – armed against any eventuality – bear their tidings at a run.

3. (opposite) Winged 'victories', such as this 'Victory of Samothrace' figure, were made to celebrate Greek military victories.

Ionian cities of the northeastern Aegean had risen in revolt against their conquerors.

If the conservative kings of Persia despised the collective spirit of the Greek cities, far more was now at stake. The independent ways of the mainland Greek cities were, the Persians felt, threatening the stability of their Asian empire. Greece, it was decided, had to be crushed – for Persia's sake. In 490 BC, Cyrus's successor, the fearsome Darius I, launched a direct attack across the Aegean. Though all Greeks found their independence threatened, it fell to democratic Athens to take the lead in their defence. The Athenians' precious liberty was in any case particularly threatened by Darius, who had brought the aged tyrant Hippias with him in the intention of re-establishing him in power. Left in the lurch by the other cities, Athens was forced to face the invaders alone, assisted only by a small troop of hoplites (citizen-soldiers) from the tiny city of Plataea. Even warlike Sparta made excuses, pleading that a religious festival prevented its soldiers from setting out to assist the Athenians before the next full moon.

1

2

1. Darius I receives the homage of a state official.

2. A disdainful camel condescends to follow its Persian driver.

Persian king Cyrus the Great's secret weapon against enemy cavalry was the camel: horses would shy away in terror, he thought, at the sight and smell of camels.

Darius landed his force of many thousands on the coastal plain of Marathon, where his cavalry would have maximum room to manoeuvre. It was too wide open a field by far for Athens's 9000-strong hoplite square, yet the Athenians marched out undaunted to do battle. The enormous cultural gulf between the two sides extended right down to the level of battlefield tactics. Athens' hoplites fought as infantry, standing shoulder to shoulder, a citizen army. For the Persian nobility facing them even to appear on foot in public was considered a disgrace. Cyrus the Great had decreed that a true Persian should ride everywhere.

To their enemy's incredulity (and perhaps their own), the Greek square gave but did not break before the impact of the Persian charge. Though outnumbered by more than two to one, they held in the centre and pushed inward from the wings. Almost surrounded now, the Persians broke and fled for the safety of their ships, leaving the Athenians in possession of the field.

The menace returns

Ten years later, in 480, the Persians were back, now under the leadership of a new king, Darius's son Xerxes. This time the Greeks presented a slightly more united front. For while the bulk of the Spartan army was once again detained by religious duties, the Spartan Leonidas with his 'Brave 300' followers maintained their city's honour by their heroism at the Thermopylae Pass. They could stem the tide of Persians streaming southward through the mountains only briefly before being ▷▷

1

1. Themistocles, saviour of his city, Athens, was fittingly commemorated by his own coin.

2. A Spartan warrior radiates warlike self-assurance.

Previous page: The destruction of Xerxes' fleet at Salamis arguably outweighed even the triumph of Marathon in military significance. Here, it is seen through the modern eyes of a 19th-century German painter.

2

overwhelmed by the sheer weight of numbers of the onrushing force, but their stand gave the Athenians time to evacuate to safety.

Led by the statesman Themistocles, the people of Athens retired to the walled port area of Piraeus to watch their beloved city burn, while the invaders looted and pillaged as they pleased. By a brilliant ruse of Themistocles, the Athenian fleet was meanwhile withdrawing to the strait of Salamis. The Persian ships, following in what they thought to be triumphant pursuit, in fact found that they were outmanoeuvred in these narrow waters. Themistocles' trap was sprung: the Greek navy completely savaged and smashed the Persian fleet. For all its apparent success, Xerxes' invasion was effectively over. Though in full possession of the prize, the Persian land force found itself stripped of its seaborne logistical support, and had no alternative but to retire, returning the smouldering city to its citizens.

Greece was saved, against all the odds, and Athenian democracy was preserved, albeit at the price of the city itself. As the Athenian general Nicias told his troops, however, this was really no cause for mourning, 'for it is men who make the polis', he said, 'not the stone and wood of its walls and buildings'. Though Athens' physical fabric lay in ruins, the city had never stood so proud as it did now, guardian of Greece and undisputed leader among Greek cities.

The following year, in 479, Persia's defeat was confirmed at the battle of Plataea, where combined Greek armies finally expelled the last of the Persian forces from mainland Greece.

CLASS WAR: THE HOPLITE

Fighting side-by-side with his neighbours in a solid square or phalanx, the Greek hoplite (citizen-soldier) was a military and political revolution. The hoplites were armed with bronze helmets (see below), long, heavy spears for thrusting, and round shields that overlapped with one another to form an impenetrable wall. Their success was a triumph of collective spirit and discipline over the individual prowess of the old warrior élite. The mounted nobility were, in fact, rendered increasingly irrelevant by the hoplites' rise: the phalanx was a significant step towards democracy in action. It was fitting, therefore, that the first great hoplite victory, at Marathon, should have been won by democratic Athens.

ATHENS ASCENDANT

ATHENS ASCENDANT

On the smoking ruins that Xerxes left, the Athenians built a beautiful new city. No power on earth could stand in the way of the people who had seen off the might of Persia. If the physical fabric of Athens had been destroyed, the spirit of its citizens had never been higher: the destruction of the city marked a coming of age for Athenian democracy. So it was that Athens faced the world full of self-confidence, its military forces victorious, its democracy triumphantly vindicated.

A golden age of achievement awaited as the Athenians led Greece in an unprecedented explosion of creativity. Classical Athens was not a museum of culture, but rather a booming commercial city, its merchants and industrialists every bit as intrepid as its architects and artists. The daring advances of Athenian philosophy were matched by the city's adventures in the field of war, the Athenians' civic pride equalled by their openness to the outside world.

Previous page: The triumph of the world's first democracy was, paradoxically, the triumph of one man. Statesman, visionary and consummate politician, Pericles presided over the 'golden age' of Athens.

THE CITY REBORN

At first a heart-rending disaster, the destruction wrought by the Persians in 480 BC was quickly seen as an opportunity. The Athenians set to with enthusiasm to rebuild their shattered city. Now they had the chance to construct their own future, to build a fit home for the people they had become: their world's pre-eminent state and, more important, its first democracy. The man who had masterminded victory in war led the city through the first years of peace: it was Themistocles who organized the rebuilding of the city walls.

Of all the Athenians, Themistocles was perhaps the most outward-looking. While others hankered after the agricultural past, for him Athens' destiny had always been as a seaport. When the attacking Persians had first been repulsed at Marathon, Themistocles urged his fellow citizens not to relax in triumph but to busy themselves building the world's biggest navy. In the glorious wake of their victory at Salamis, Athenians had cause to be thankful that they had heeded his advice, and they readily accepted Themistocles's leadership. His priorities remained unchanged. The new fortifications he devised included a corridor some 8 km (5 miles) long, binding Athens and Piraeus, its port, into a single built-up area. Ensuring that Athens' seaborne supplies would be protected in the event of another war, the 'Long Wall' had an equally significant, if less obvious, intention. The whole emphasis of the state was subtly changed by Themistocles's scheme: no longer a landward-looking agricultural polis, Athens was now a maritime, mercantile city.

1. Even in ruins a splendid sight, the new civic centre the Athenians built has stood as a symbol of Greek civilization ever since.

1

2

The Acropolis transformed

It had been Themistocles's intention to leave the destruction on the Acropolis as it was, as a monument to what Greeks saw as the savagery of their Persian enemies. But such a negative aspiration could not last long in these ebullient times, and soon another statesman came to the fore with more ambitious plans – Pericles, whose name became virtually synonymous with Athens's golden age.

Pericles's great construction project gave him the chance to construct himself a career as undisputed 'first citizen' of the foremost city of the world. By 449 BC he was leading Athens in an awesome programme of public building – graceful temples, imposing courts and council chambers, splendid monuments. Though, as befitted a democratic city, the centre of activities had shifted down from the heights of the Acropolis to the open Agora below, the hilltop became the stage for a stupendous symbolic display of civic power.

Pride of place was taken by the Parthenon, Athena's temple: in its astonishing symmetry, it was the ultimate expression of the 'classical' spirit, a vast mass of marble riding on slender columns. Within the temple stood a statue of Athena in gold and ivory some 11 m (35 ft) high. Across the hilltop all around stretched a stunning array of religious buildings picked out and punctuated by magnificent statues, the whole incredible complex the vision – and in some cases actually the work – of the sculptor Phidias.

Today, a symphony in shimmering whiteness, these works would all have been elaborately painted

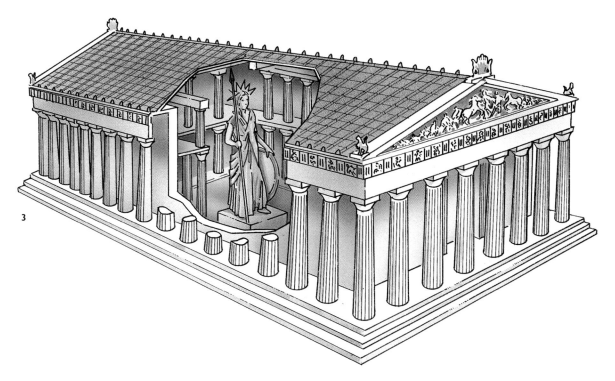

3

at the time – a riot of colour belying the modern stereotype of 'classical restraint'. Our view of the ancient Athenians as lovers of beauty is, however, abundantly attested here. Craftsmen lavished care on beautiful details high up on elevated friezes where none but the gods could ever be expected to see them.

If these public works proclaimed Athens's greatness to the heavens, Pericles's agenda was more down to earth: his programme provided a huge boost to the city's economy. For the craftsmen and labourers who built it all, as well as the carters and seafarers who supplied them, the scheme was nothing less than a 'new deal', assuring a prosperity that trickled down to every level of society.

1. Artemis, in moon-white marble, looks down from the Parthenon frieze.

2. Riders processing to the Parthenon to honour Athena in a carving taken from the Parthenon.

3. Phidias's awe-inspiring statue of Athena would have dominated the space inside the goddess's temple, the Parthenon, built in 447–432 BC.

⭐ Despite its achievements, Athens struggled to feed itself: the crime of exporting corn was punishable by death.

The heart of Athens: the Agora

The Agora, meanwhile, was becoming the bustling heart of democratic Athens in the mid-5th century BC. Its political, judicial, religious, commercial and social life all found a focus here. In a new *bouleterion* (council-chamber) the elected assembly met to discuss the civic issues of the day, while Athenians who fell foul of the law found themselves being judged by juries of their own fellow citizens in the adjacent lawcourts. In the southeast corner of the Agora a mint cast coins on the people's authority, and the nearby streets seem to have been the centre for the city's bronze-casting trade. On raised ground overlooking the open area was the temple to Hephaistos. God of metalworking and male counterpart to Athena as divine patron of the city, his shrine did honour to the heritage of Athens'

past with a series of sculptures commemorating the deeds of Theseus, slayer of the Minotaur and the city's legendary ruler. An assortment of smaller shrines – to Apollo, Zeus and others – helped make this area the centre of the city's ritual life, just as a series of *stoas* (colonnaded porticoes) concentrated commercial and social activity.

Citizens would leave their workshops and warehouses in the surrounding streets to idle away their leisure hours in the many barbershops and taverns the stoas housed – or simply to stroll down their long arcades through the throng of market-stalls, pestered by pedlars and entertained by acrobats and clowns as they chatted with friends or business contacts. From butchers to blacksmiths, from onion-sellers to cobblers, every imaginable trade was represented in and around the Athenian Agora. To enforce trading standards, discourage

1. Trees and stalls punctuate the open area of the agora, the centre of Athenian life.

1

thieves and swindlers and prevent squabbles from breaking out over pitches, a permanent staff of *agoranomoi* was employed.

Just another class of tradesmen, philosophers set up shop here, their wide-ranging conversation with their students an education in itself. Philosophy had been a vital aspect of Greek cultural life ever since wandering teachers like Xenophanes started questioning the nature of being in the late 6th century BC. His scepticism towards what he regarded as the superstitious credulity of people who worshipped the Olympian gods set the standard of rationalism for philosophers for ever afterwards. By the beginning of the 5th century, the Sophists, with their dazzling facility for arguing both sides of any given case, were developing skills that would be invaluable in Greek political life as well as demonstrating the shifty elusiveness of truth. The term 'sophistry' is today applied to clever but unscrupulous intellectual argument, but the usage does these brilliant, searching thinkers a grave injustice. Later in the 5th century, the dialogues held in the Athenian Agora between Socrates and his pupils, as recorded by Plato, provided the basis for the whole history of Western thought. Add in the later contribution of one of Plato's students, Aristotle, some would say, and all the essentials of modern philosophy were in place. Another later philosophical movement, Stoicism, would take its name from Athens's *stoa poikile* (painted stoa), where its teachers and adherents met to walk and talk. To 'live in conformance with nature' was the Stoics' aim: they took a logical, materialistic view of life – their god was Reason.

2

3

2. The Erechtheion shrine marked the spot on which Athena was believed to have founded her city.

3. Athens's warlike achievements found both commemoration and inspiration in the temple of Athena Nike.

A GOLDEN AGE OF CULTURE

The great public projects of Periclean Athens (449–31 BC) were only the most obvious, large-scale features of an artistic outpouring arguably without rival before or since. For the graceful simplicities of classical art are as readily to be traced in the delicate curve of a terracotta vase as in the soaring columns and massive pediment of the greatest temple. The effect is much the same in each, architectural mastery matching ceramic expertise in capturing a sense of effortless ease, invigorating inert clay and solid stone alike.

In its essentials the artistic output of classical Greece does not differ all that much from that of the age preceding it, yet to the modern observer the breakthrough could hardly be more striking. Technical and aesthetic developments that had been taking place over decades and centuries came together at this time to such an extent that Greek art attained some sort of collective lift-off. What had been round, squat vessels seemed to stretch out into elegance; stolid columns grew slender as they reached for the sky; above all, the human form was caught in unprecedented vitality. Grand and impressive the old statuary may have been, but in the work of the 5th century we find something new: a sense of pulsating life, of human scale. The animation some sculptors were breathing into cold marble, others were casting into molten bronze, while artists conjured up comparable effects in everything from the tiniest ceramic motifs to the largest wall-paintings. Yet, while such 'plastic' (moulded or modelled) arts have stood the test of

1

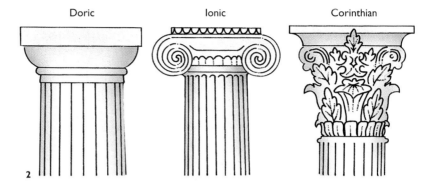

Doric   Ionic   Corinthian

1. Dating from around 100 BC, the 'Venus de Milo' sculpture depicts Aphrodite, goddess of love, under her Roman title.

2. Greek columns sprouted extra ornamentation as the classical age wore on.

time particularly well, the classical achievement was certainly not confined to these disciplines. This was an age of innovation and miraculous attainment in every cultural field.

Dramatic developments

Greek drama – Greek tragedy in particular – is regarded as one of the timeless glories of the classical achievement, yet the few surviving texts give no hint of the real richness of the ancient Athenian theatre. The great tragedies of Aeschylus, Sophocles and Euripides, the comedies of Aristophanes: these formed only a small part of lavish – and by modern standards peculiarly ill-sorted – programmes of entertainment. For the god Dionysos, in whose name the original Greek dramas were enacted every year, was associated not only with fertility but with drunken ribaldry, song and religious ecstasy. Drama both high and low therefore fell naturally to Dionysos's brief, as did stately processions, smutty jokes and wild carousing. The conjunction may seem strange to us, but to the ancient Greeks it was not only logical

but compelling. Athens alone celebrated seven Dionysian festivals annually. The entire populace had their roles in these great productions, for which the whole city served as a stage, while – perhaps accompanied by a raucous band – priests and civic dignitaries led the noisy progress to the theatre.

Nestling in the natural folds of the hillside, just below the summit of the Acropolis, the Athenian theatre was a huge auditorium whose terraced stone seating could accommodate an audience of some 17,000. To judge by surviving classical Greek theatres, such as the equivalently sized one at Epidaurus in the Peloponnese, it may have had a surprisingly intimate feel for all its enormous size. At Epidaurus, it has been found that a spectator seated right at the back in the topmost row, could have heard a mere whisper on the stage below. The actors' voices were in any case assisted by the masks they wore, which have been shown to serve also as megaphones. Their primary purpose, though, was to project visually to even the most distant circle of the auditorium the essential qualities of the character represented: not just their rank and gender, but their prevailing   ▷▷

1

2

1. Though roofed in at the rear with semi-permanent structures for entrances and exits, the classical stage was essentially a simple space, with very little in the way of scenery.

2. The faultless sightlines and astonishing acoustics made theatres like Epidaurus the perfect place to watch a play.

3. (opposite) The grotesque masks worn by these strolling actors give a sense of the abrasiveness that characterized Greek comedy.

1. A girl dances to the music of a wind instrument in this painting from a 5th-century BC goblet.

2. The actors in this theatrical scene wear the standard comic actors' padded clothing and mask.

emotion, too. The great plays of the 5th-century BC dramatists, which we now see performed in their isolation, in fact formed only sections in long and diverse programmes: music and dance were very likely as important as actual drama. First, however, cattle and grain had to be offered in sacrifice to Dionysos by his priests, libations of wine poured in his name, and the god's blessing sought for the city and its festival. Then children orphaned in war would traditionally be paraded for public sympathy and outrage before events took what we would recognize as their first truly dramatic turn.

Along with austere tragedies, recounting the terrible downfalls of past heroes and kings, there were satirical comedies in which public figures of the time were irreverently – even viciously – ridiculed. Wildest of all were the satyr plays in which actors in animal costumes enacted the earthiest of farces. Greek tragedy seems such rarefied fare now, it is hard for us to imagine the popular spirit in which it was originally enjoyed. At the time, it was a competitive event – almost a spectator sport. Three dramatists would be entered at a typical festival, each vying with the others for the victor's prize, and each perhaps contributing three full-length tragedies and a satyr play. By the standards of modern theatregoers this would appear a gruelling schedule, but the Greek theatre seems to have been beloved of all, from the wealthy and educated to the humblest artisans. Even slaves and prisoners were often allowed their freedom for the day to come and participate in this, the most genuinely democratic of Athenian festivals.   ▷▷

3

BUILDERS OF DEMOCRACY

Archaeologists excavating the Acropolis in the 19th century unearthed a series of stone slabs on which some builders' accounts had been inscribed. Covering work on just one temple for a single year, 409 BC, these still ran to 2650 closely written lines. Expenses for sacrifices were recorded, along with supplies such as gold leaf, lead, guttering and oil. Numerous different categories of workers were carefully listed: carpenters, stonemasons, gilders, painters, scaffolders and hoist operators – not to mention the sculptors who did the decorative work. Citizens, slaves and metics worked side by side for equal pay (though slaves had to hand theirs over to their masters). These accounts make graphically clear how public projects had such a galvanizing effect throughout the entire Athenian economy.

3. Six maidens, their slightness belying their structural importance, bear up the southern portico of the Erechtheion shrine.

1

2

3

TRAINING MIND AND BODY

Physical and mental fitness were inseparable for the ancient Greeks, and the school or 'gymnasion' trained both mind and body. The philosophers initially set up in the agora, but later they transferred their operations out into the suburbs, where there was space for a more integrated approach to education. In addition to sheltered walks for strolling and talking, Plato's famous Academy had running tracks and a sports arena. The importance of athletic accomplishments had been enshrined in Greek culture since the inauguration of the games at Olympia in the western Peloponnese some time before the 8th century BC.

5

1. A long-jumper lands, watched by officials.

2. Greek boxers confront one another toe to toe.

3. Runners near the turning-post (far left) in a long-distance race.

4. An athlete summons up all his concentration as he makes ready to hurl a discus.

5. Wrestlers vie for advantage.

THE LIMITS OF FREEDOM

The Athenian citizen had a degree of direct involvement in the daily government of his state that makes modern claims of democracy ring a little hollow. Instead of casting a single vote every few years to elect an all-powerful executive that might otherwise ignore him, he could take his views to his fellow-citizens whenever he liked. Though a large elected senate took care of the most workaday decisions, the entire electorate assembled frequently to establish public opinion on specific issues. But if Athenian democracy puts its modern equivalent to shame in some respects, in others its limitations are only too obvious. The liberties enjoyed by the citizens of Athens coexisted with the disenfranchisement of many thousands. Arguably, indeed, the Athenians's freedom and prosperity could not have been maintained without the enslavement of others.

A long way from liberty

In the hills to the southwest of Athens was the state-owned silver mine at Laurion – big finds of silver at Laurion would get the city out of difficulties more than once. Here, in conditions of indescribable hardship and fearful danger, men worked in narrow and tortuous tunnels as much as 100 m (320 ft) down. The miners would have been surprised to learn that they served one of the world's greatest civilizations. No one would ever have worked here of his own free will. Apart from convicted criminals, most of the labourers were

DECEPTIVE SYMMETRIES

Classical Greek architecture awes us by its con-summate regularity, and by the perfect balance in which it is conceived and built. Yet modern research has revealed a more anarchic side to this order – one in which not the architect's intelligence but the builders' skills were at the fore. Investigation into the construction of Athenian temples suggests that individual craftsmen were given enormous scope for improvisation: the architect gave his men only the sketchiest idea of his conception. This makes even more incredible the extent to which infinitesimal irregularities have been built into apparently sym-metrical buildings to accommodate the minutest distortions of the human eye. The 'straight' upper step on which the Parthenon rests, for example, curves up at the corners by 230 mm (9 in), one-thousandth of its length, while the columns bulge by 18 mm (0.75 in) two-fifths of the way up. The 'perfection' of the Parthenon (shown below in a 19th-century watercolour) is thus attained by a series of controlled 'mistakes' – all estimated with unerring accuracy by its ancient builders.

slaves – but there were more of these, it has been estimated, than there were citizens in the whole of the city of Athens.

Within the city itself, it is thought, a free population of 150,000 was served by a further 100,000 slaves. These had been bought on the international market, brought home as prisoners of war – or of course born into the condition of slavery in Athens itself. They were not necessarily worked to death as ruthlessly as their fellows at Laurion, though much of the most arduous physical labour was certainly performed by slaves. While many were domestic servants, others worked alongside freemen in occupations both menial and skilled: their condition was outwardly identical with that of their freeborn workmates – except that, when payday came, their wages went directly to their masters. Slaves with valued skills or education might even live better than poor citizens in material terms – but whatever their comforts, they did not have their freedom, nor any voice in the running of their city.

Free, yet foreign

Freeborn foreigners or 'metics' may at some periods have constituted up to 40 per cent of the population. Though non-Athenian, they were often Greek, so they assimilated easily. Speaking the language and sharing the culture, such metics might rise high in business and move in the most exalted social circles, though the privileges of citizenship would always be denied them. As the 5th century BC gave way to the 4th, and Athens's

1

2

1. The owl, denoting wisdom, was Athena's symbol. Here the owl is depicted on a coin of her city, Athens.

2. A physician treats a patient in ancient Athens.

1. In this terracotta model a woman prepares a meal.

2. The Greek ideal in feminine beauty personified, the bride Thalea makes ready for her wedding. Glauke, attending, brings a necklace to complete the effect in this vase-painting from the 5th century BC.

3. Another vase, another section of society: a laundress labours hard for a meagre living.

trade with the world continued to thrive, the number of 'barbarian' foreigners in the city grew accordingly. Named for the 'bar-bar-bar-bar' babble of their incomprehensible tongues, the barbarians included any non-Greek outsider: in 4th-century Athens that mainly meant Thracians from the southern Balkans and Lydians and Carians from western Asia Minor, in addition to Phoenicians and Egyptians and many others. These metics, too,

might do well for themselves – the brothers Lysias and Polemarchos from the Greek colony of Syracuse in Sicily employed 120 slaves in their weapons factory and appear to have been accepted into the most exclusive sections of Athenian society. But most metics made little effort to adapt their manners and customs to the ways of a state which, tolerant as it was, showed no signs of rewarding them with citizenship.

A woman's place

Women had no political status in ancient Athens. A woman's place was in the home. Even there, it was assumed that she would be seen rather than heard: a submissive silence was the mark of a woman's modesty. Men's complete authority over their womenfolk was written into the law, but that was not the only source of their domestic power – for the most part they were much older than their wives. As girls were considered grown-up from the very moment they reached puberty, they might easily be as young as 12 or 13 when they were married. The well-born Athenian woman might have found much to envy in the lot of her inferiors. Poor families could not afford the regime of honour that kept rich wives housebound. Women from the lower orders found work as nurses, midwives, laundresses, textile-workers, craftswomen and small traders. One female occupation that cut across all social boundaries was prostitution: from street whores to glamorous courtesans, prostitutes were an indispensable aspect of Athenian life.

The family was first and foremost an economic unit: wives bore sons to inherit their father's wealth and daughters to trade for dynastic connections. While many marriages may well have grown into loyal friendships, Athenian men did not look to their wives for intellectual companionship, or even sexual fulfilment: for this they went to prostitutes – or their male acquaintances. Homosexuality was not the exclusive orientation it tends to be today. 'Greek love', as it has been called, was an addition, rather than an alternative, to marriage.

3

Classical Athens was not a large city by modern standards, with, at most, a quarter of a million inhabitants.

1

MEANWHILE IN SPARTA ...

So clamorously have the achievements of classical Athens resounded down the centuries that it is easy to forget it is not the whole Greek story. Though all Greeks shared in the benefits of Athens's cultural revolution – artefacts from throughout Greece display a new adventurousness, a new confidence at this time – many city-states held aloof from what they regarded as a dangerous experiment.

Chief among the dissenters was the military state of Sparta, which held much of the Peloponnese in domination. This was ironic, given that the Spartan system had in its day been among the more progressive in Greece. Renowned for their valour and feared for their harshness, the Spartans prided themselves on their independent ways. Long before the Athenians overthrew their oppressive aristocracy, the Spartans resolved their own internal tensions in a novel way. Annexing the neighbouring state of Messenia, they bound its population into servitude as serfs or 'helots', and set them to work on Spartan land. Not quite slaves, but not freemen either, the helots had to hand over to their masters 50 per cent of what they produced. Their labour liberated even the poorest Spartan citizen from the necessity of having to work to support themselves.

Previous page:
Seen here in terracotta,
women playing
knucklebones: a familiar
feature of the ancient
Athenian scene.

1. A girl carries a comedy
mask in statuette – though
in the real theatre all roles
would have been taken by
male actors.

Every Spartan was free, but caught up from cradle to grave in a military discipline that would not in reality have allowed him a moment's liberty of thought or movement. Boys were taken from their mothers at the age of seven, and enrolled in paramilitary 'packs' to be brought up by adult men and older boys. From the age of 12 they lived communally, under military conditions; bullying and abuse were encouraged as part of the toughening process. Systematically underfed, and inadequately clothed and shod for the rigours of the mountain winter, they grew up hardy and physically self-reliant, though with little sense of any personal identity beyond that which the state invested in them as soldiers.

Girls, too, were taken from their parents and brought up tough on a regime of unrelenting physical exercise. Running and dancing naked, and mixing easily with the Spartan boys, their lack of inhibition scandalized visitors from other Greek cities. Such freedoms as they enjoyed, however, existed in a context of near-total institutionalization. Like their male peers, they lived highly regimented lives, and would have known little of individuality or personal liberty.

But if Sparta gave its citizens discipline rather than democracy, it was a system under which all felt equal, and were bound by an indomitable spirit of comradeship. Though freedom of the individual would have meant little to them, they had a strong sense of the sovereignty of the state. Thus Sparta had come to Athens's assistance in the struggle against the tyranny of Peisistratos and his sons, however little it can have liked the radical reforms

GREEK SCIENCE

Nowhere do the Greeks seem less 'ancient' than in their explorations into science. Where other civilizations accepted the universe as divinely ordained and not to be questioned by mere mortals, the Greeks enquired constantly into just how creation worked. They established the studies of botany, zoology and geology and took mathematics and physics to levels that would not be matched until the European Renaissance of the 16th century AD. Not that the Greeks saw science as we do: for them, the spheres of science, philosophy and religion came together. The mathematical theorems of Pythagoras (born c. 580 BC – depicted on a coin below) are still very much in use today, but he also pronounced mystical doctrines that often seem bizarre to us.

for which its intervention helped clear the way. Sparta's snub to the Athenians before Marathon in 490 BC (▷ p.45) almost certainly reflects its mixed feelings about the system it was being called upon to help defend – at the same time, of course, the prospect of a rival's defeat would not have been displeasing to the Spartans. In the end, by its most unmilitary vacillation before the battle of Marathon, Sparta succeeded only in handing the political initiative to Athens, which emerged from the war Greece's undisputed leader.

A tremor shakes Sparta

A massive earthquake in 465 BC caused widespread destruction throughout Sparta, but the political aftershocks were, if anything, more devastating still. Independent to the point of introversion, Sparta had shown less interest than the other Greek cities in overseas trade. The damage its agricultural system sustained in the earthquake thus went straight to the heart of its economy. In the ensuing crisis, the helots saw their chance to rise up in rebellion. The unrest lasted for 10 years before it was finally put down. The effort involved in doing so imposed other internal strains on a state that was already feeling the humiliation resulting from

1. (opposite) Spartan girls had to be as tough as their male counterparts, as this athletic figure from the 6th century BC vividly shows.

Athenian success. Setting itself squarely against democratization, the Spartan state could not insulate itself entirely against the unsettling effects of the Athenian experiment on its own lower classes. And if poorer Spartans were restless, so too were neighbouring states who saw in Sparta's nervousness a chance to end the long years of its ascendancy in the Peloponnesian peninsula.

The Theban strategy

Another conservative state, Thebes, the major city of Boeotia in central Greece, tried different tactics at different times to avoid being sucked into the spiral of radical reform it saw taking place in Athens. Towards the end of the 6th century BC and in the early decades of the 5th century, the Thebans had flirted with the Persian emperors, their fear of the foreigner less than their dread of internal political unrest. Like many of the more northerly cities in Greece, Thebes had seen the Persians both as threat and as protection. While menacing the sovereignty of the Greek states, the Persians' dominance at least assured the continuation of the old aristocratic rule in these cities. In return for such ready cooperation, the Persians could afford to be magnanimous. Thebes and the other cities were never attacked by force in the way their more southerly neighbours were. The Athenian victory at Marathon, however, saw this diplomatic strategy brought to an ignominious end. Rather than throw in their lot with the victorious democracy, Thebes's rulers preferred to enter into a new alliance with the Athenians' Spartan foes.

THE DECLINE OF DEMOCRACY

THE DECLINE OF DEMOCRACY

As the 5th century BC wore on and Athens only grew in glory, other Greek cities felt themselves increasingly pushed to the political margins. While all to some extent shared the benefits of the classical miracle, Athens's increasing ascendancy was resented – not only by those conservative states, such as Sparta, which had been distrustful from the start. Even some of Athens's allies were at odds with a state whose concern for its own liberties seemed to preclude any recognition of the rights of other cities.

For the Athenians, democracy seemed to begin and end at home. This proved in time to be the tragic flaw that brought the city crashing down from its incredible eminence. From this time on, the Athenian story was a tale of amazing attainments slowly unravelling, as a power that had come to feel entitled to supremacy as of right found itself ill-equipped to maintain its hold over other states with other values, other ideas.

Previous page: Greek soldiers and a Persian cavalryman clash in this vase-painting from the 5th century BC. From this time forward, Greek would often be pitched against Greek in war.

OVERSHADOWED BY ATHENS

Other Greek cities envied Athens's power and prosperity and feared its increasingly arrogant ways. Even Athens's closest allies came to chafe under its domination. The Delian League was established in 479 BC as an alliance of the Greek islands and seafaring cities against the possibility of another Persian invasion. In theory centred on the sacred island of Delos, birthplace of both Apollo and Artemis, the League had grown into what amounted to an Athenian empire. Supposedly just the first among equal partners, Athens was far and away the richest and strongest state: the conduct of the League became an excuse to bully the smaller cities for tribute. When in 470 BC the island of Naxos attempted to leave the alliance, all pretence of partnership was dropped: the Athenian fleet blockaded the rebels and forced them back into line.

In the years that followed there were several more attempts to escape a bond that was becoming more irksome. The Athenian response was invariably uncompromising – and often violent. With the Persian threat receding ever further into the past, the League's original justification was melting away with each passing year, and its continuance was regarded with mounting cynicism by its smaller members. By the mid-5th century BC, Athens' politicians hardly bothered to pretend that they invested League revenues in men and ships for the defence of all. Instead, they blatantly spent the loot on their own self-advertising building projects. Flushed with its new-found wealth and power, Athens complacently ignored the rising resentment.

1. The ruined 'House of Cleopatra' on Delos. Supposedly the centre of the Delian League, Delos was, in fact, no more than a pawn in the Athenian game.

2. This magnificent lion stands guard over the god Apollo's shrine on the island of Delos, revered by the ancient Greeks as Apollo's birthplace.

The Peloponnesian problem

As discontent festered among sometime friends, so too did the rancour of old enemies. Taken together, these two trends represented grave peril for Athens. But so heady was the city's success that none could imagine the good times ending. Athens would continue, it seemed, to surge from strength to strength. Having smashed the Persian fleet once and for all at the Eurymedon river in 469 BC, Athens managed to place a puppet ruler in Egypt in 460, assuring itself sole charge of what had previously been a Persian granary. Only six years later, however, a Persian admiral defeated the Athenian fleet there, seizing back Egypt – with all its grain – for his emperor. That same year, after a decade's attrition, Sparta succeeded in bringing its helot insurgency to an end.

Suddenly the world was beginning to look a much more dangerous, unpredictable place, but Athens was slow to read the warning signs. Even when Sparta, at the head of its own Peloponnesian League, began to take a more belligerent line, Athens' complacency remained unruffled. In 431 BC, the two rival power blocs, headed respectively by Athens and Sparta, went to war. The conflict would continue for 27 years.

War had been part of the Greek way of life for centuries, but battles tended to be short, highly ritualized bouts between hoplite phalanxes with relatively few casualties on either side. Strictly a seasonal, summer occupation, it was unheard of for war between Greek states to go on beyond a few weeks' campaigning. Though the victors might make off with the losers' cattle and crops, the

1. Two hoplite soldiers confront each other in a 5th-century BC vase-painting that seems to sum up the Greek situation in a time of mounting conflict.

2. A desperate defender sallies forth from a city under siege in a relief carved at the very end of the Peloponnesian War.

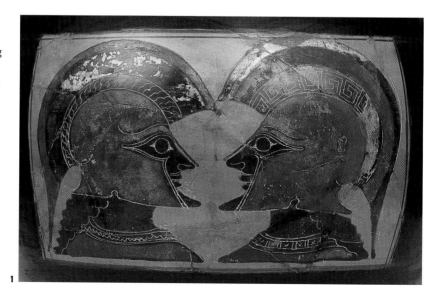

1

economic impact of such skirmishing was slight. By the time of the Peloponnesian War, however, with the armies of numerous allies doing battle at different times across a wide geographical area, the effects were cumulatively exhausting. Athens in particular was damaged by the war. Pericles's handling of strategy was disastrous from the start. Evacuating the farming people from the countryside around Athens and bringing them inside the city walls, he let the Spartan forces roam unopposed,

laying waste to the region's fields and vineyards. Far from tiring the invaders out, this plan only raised their confidence sky-high, while Athenians, cowering within their city, were thoroughly demoralized. Their agricultural economy in ruins, the campaign at sea apparently going nowhere, the Athenians' woes were crowned by the onset of an epidemic of plague. Crammed together, the Athenians succumbed to the disease in their thousands. By 429, it is thought, a quarter of the population had died.

▷ THE GREEK GUERRILLAS

At close quarters on open ground, to which it was ideally suited, the hoplite phalanx was an intimidating sight. But on hillsides and in narrow mountain passes, its solidity and discipline could make it vulnerable. As the Peloponnesian War went on, military leaders on both sides returned to older, less sophisticated ways of war, sending out a variety of lightly armed troops – archers, javelin-throwers, slingers and even stone-throwers – to harry their enemies in rugged terrain.

1. A warlike myth for a warlike age: Greeks and Amazon warrior women fight to the death.

2. Strongman of the Macedonian mountains, Philip brought all Greece under his sway.

1

The golden age ends

Pericles himself died in 429 BC, another victim of the plague – his death only underlining the fact that the golden age was over. That idea would have been derided by the citizens of what was still Greece's greatest city: Athenian decline, when it came, was slow enough to be all but imperceptible. But the fact remains that the future held an apparently unending war of attrition. Not that Athens's plight was entirely of its enemies' making. In the Assembly, rival factions fought back and forth for authority: Creon and his followers proclaiming a proud sense of Athenian tradition; Alcibiades and his 'young progressives' conjuring up a vision of achievements

yet in store. Meanwhile, the city drifted, effectively leaderless. Many were relieved when, in 411 BC and again in 404, military juntas seized power. Neither lasted long, however, and wrapped up in its own political in-fighting, Athens let slip several chances to agree a negotiated peace with a Peloponnesian League that itself began to flag. And so the conflict lurched on until, in 405 BC, Athens lost its long-standing control of the sea when the Spartans destroyed its fleet at Aegostami, Asia Minor, cutting off Athens itself from seaborne supplies. Conditions became truly desperate as the Spartan army tightened the noose around the city, with no food now coming in from any side. In 404 BC the Athenians surrendered, their power broken.

RE-ENTER THE TYRANT

Almost three decades of war had taken their toll on the Greek cities. Sparta gained little from its victory. Its dominance came to be as bitterly resented as that of Athens had been, and it wore itself out in a long struggle for supremacy with its Theban former allies. Thebes, coming to the fore in its turn, proved no more effective in the leadership role. With no state strong enough to take pre-eminence, a power vacuum was created into which Philip of Macedon was only too ready to move. Ruler of what until now had been an insignificant kingdom in the mountainous north of mainland Greece, Philip saw his opportunity in the depletion of the southern city-states. A skilled and unscrupulous operator, he had no compunction in having his Macedonian rivals murdered; he was no less ruthless in his dealings with neighbouring powers. Yet he was never the royal thug his enemies in Greece liked to imagine. A cunning diplomat, at times even charming, he was all too easily underestimated. By the middle of the 4th century, the Greek cities were just waking up to the fact that an imperial power was growing up on their northern doorstep. The realization came too late for Philip to be stopped.

2

A forceful negotiator

Philip was a tireless diplomat who seems to have seen negotiation mainly as a way of buying himself time, of lulling his enemies into delusive calm while he quietly outmanoeuvred them. Diplomacy for the Macedonian tyrant was in any case inseparable

> ⭐ Philip ensured his armies' 'courage' in the most effective way: by stationing cavalry behind their lines to kill any deserters.

from the threat of force – a threat his Macedonian armies were becoming ever better equipped to deliver on. When Philip had first seized power in Pellas in 359 BC, Macedonians had been vaguely feared as barbaric savages, hardy mountain folk not much softened by civilization. It was one thing to be wild, another to be a formidable fighting force, which is what Philip's root-and-branch reforms in the Macedonian military now created. In the first place he established a permanent, professional army – not an *ad hoc* collection of conscripts assembled seasonally as in previous times – training them up to a new and fearsome way of waging war. Beefing up the Greek-style phalanx (▷ p.49), he equipped

his hoplite soldiers with the dreaded sarissa (Macedonian pike). This was almost twice as long as the traditional hoplite weapon and far more penetrating. Opposing infantry, with shorter spears, could not engage closely enough to inflict injury. As long as they kept in close formation, Philip's phalanx had little to fear from any Greek enemy: daily drills ensured an awesome level of discipline. Philip's trademark tactic in battle was the embolos, or wedge-formation. His infantry engaged the enemy front line not head-on but at an angle. Their assault opened a cleft into which the Macedonian cavalry would then pour at a gallop, their attack going right to the heart of the enemy square.

 UNWORTHY OF THEIR FREEDOM

Berating his fellow Greeks for their acquiescence in Philip's tyranny, the great Athenian orator Demosthenes (see right) said that they themselves, not the dictator, must take the blame. 'There was one advantage, gentle-men,' he said, 'which lay in Philip's hands. Among the Greek states, not in isolated instances but everywhere, there came into existence a crop of corrupt, abominable traitors beyond all previous memory. With them as accomplices and collaborators he worked on the deteriorating condition of the Greeks and their internal dissensions, and made these worse… No one would dare to breathe the idea that it was fitting for a man born and bred in a small, mean city like Pellas to have in him such greatness of spirit as to set in his heart the desire and ambition of power over Greece, while we Athenians, who every day in every word we speak, in every spectacle we look on, keep in our minds the memory of noble ancestors, should have in us a spirit so demeaned as by our own offer, our own will, to cede Philip the place of liberty…'

Victory and assassination

While Philip built his empire in the north, the Greek city-states looked on as though hypnotized to helplessness, too riven by their own mutual squabbles and internal tensions to mount any sort of serious opposition. Though all could see the danger, none could provide the leadership required. Once a source of strength, the independence of the Greek states was now only too clearly a cause of weakness. Athenian democracy, meanwhile, the system which had led Greece to its great triumph over the Persians, seemed able to offer only in-fighting and indecision.

Two rival factions arose in Athens, one in favour of aggressive resistance to Macedonian expansion, the other hoping to buy off the tyrant with meek cooperation. Philip himself worked dexterously in the diplomatic background to encourage divisions he knew would advantage him in the end. The weaker his enemy, the less work his armies would have to do. In 344 BC Philip decided he had bided his time long enough, and began to move his forces steadily southwards. Galvanized too late into unified action, Athens and Thebes patched up their quarrels to assume the lead in the Greek defence, but their forces were comprehensively smashed at the battle of Chaeronea in 338 BC.

Philip's great victory left him Greece's undisputed leader, but his rule had nothing in common with the democratic ways of old. Even those cities that spurned the Athenian way of citizen government had prized their own autonomy: now individuals and states alike were

1. Olympias, mother of Alexander, may have been a match for her son in ruthlessness.

beneath the heel of a single, absolute dictator. What seems shocking in historical hindsight is the sub-missive spirit in which the Greeks accepted their subjection. In the years that followed Philip's conquests, his new subjects do not appear to have given him a moment's trouble.

If Philip had difficulties to deal with, they originated much nearer home, where he began to suspect his own Queen Olympias, and their son Alexander, of plotting against him. Whether they really represented a threat there is no way of knowing now, but Philip – characteristically ruthless – left nothing to chance. In one swoop divorcing his wife and disowning his son, he remarried and set about starting a second royal family. This strategy fell flat when his new queen bore him a bouncing – but dynastically useless – baby girl. Philip's continuing attempts to outmanoeuvre his son may in themselves have ended up forcing the young man's hand: in 336 BC, Philip was assassinated by one of his own bodyguards. Alexander had the backing of the Macedonian army, and succeeded him unopposed.

THE AMAZING ALEXANDER

At 20, Alexander found himself supreme ruler of what was already a respectably sized empire. More important, though, he was master of what was possibly the best-trained and best-organized army the world had ever seen. Once firmly established as lord of Greece, Philip had dreamt of eastern conquests; before his death he had been building up his forces to just this purpose, but it was his son who reaped the benefits in the years that followed.

First Alexander had to get his own Macedonian house in order, suppressing the discontent that followed Philip's suspicious death. That done – and with a thoroughness his father would certainly have admired – Alexander lost no time in pushing eastwards, landing an expeditionary force in Asia Minor in 334 BC. With 32,000 infantry and 5000 cavalry, his force was substantial but by no means enormous. Thanks to Philip's training and tactical innovations, though, they were a match for a much larger army. Alexander had soldiering in his blood; he learned from his father's example, and had seen action in the thick of things at Chaeronea. He also had an instinctive understanding of warfare that made him perhaps the most successful general in history. Outmanoeuvring the Persians in their first encounter on the banks of the Granicus river, his forces surrounded the enemy and massacred them, with the loss of only 115 of their own men.

Having laid claim to the whole of Asia Minor, Alexander pressed southward into Syria the following year. At Issus, on the coast of the Mediterranean, his men prevailed again, though

1

Alexander in his travels created no fewer than 20 cities called Alexandria; he also named one city after Bucephalus, his beloved horse.

1. Youthful grace combines with determination in this Roman bust of Alexander, great soldier-king.

2. Darius's chariots were ineffectual against the well-drilled army of Alexander.

3. Southeastern Europe, Africa, Asia: Alexander's campaign of conquest took him across much of the ancient world.

2

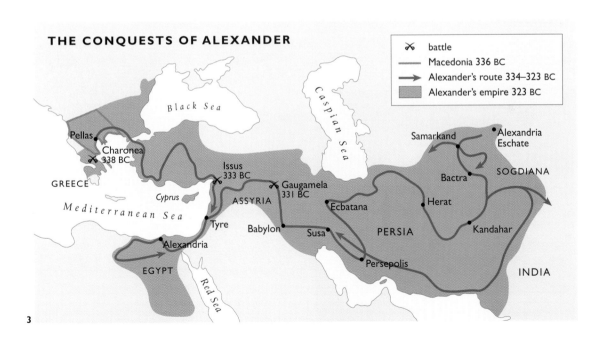

THE CONQUESTS OF ALEXANDER

⚔ battle
— Macedonia 336 BC
→ Alexander's route 334–323 BC
▓ Alexander's empire 323 BC

Black Sea

Caspian Sea

Pellas
Charonea
⚔ 338 BC
GREECE
Cyprus
Mediterranean Sea
Issus
333 BC
⚔ Gaugamela
331 BC
ASSYRIA
Ecbatana
Tyre
Babylon
Susa
Alexandria
EGYPT
Red Sea
Persepolis
PERSIA
Herat
Samarkand
Alexandria
Eschate
Bactra
SOGDIANA
Kandahar
INDIA

3

outnumbered two-to-one by the Persians. The Persian king Darius III attempted to come to terms, offering the young Macedonian his entire empire west of the Euphrates. But Alexander was having none of it, determining to take the whole of the Persian empire for himself. Before he turned his attentions eastward, however, he wanted to destroy Persia as a Mediterranean naval power. Working his way down the coast of what are now Lebanon and Israel, he besieged and conquered the main Persian ports of Tyre and Gaza. The road now lay open into Egypt where, in 332 BC, he arrived in triumph.

East meets west

No reliable documentary evidence corroborates the tradition that Alexander was crowned pharaoh in Memphis. It is appealing to think that, after so many centuries of separate development, Greece

was coming back into contact with its Middle Eastern cultural roots. Moreover, it would be in keeping with Alexander's character to respect Egyptian titles: he is certainly known to have sacrificed to the Egyptian gods. While he may have come as a brutal conqueror, Alexander always took care to honour local customs wherever he went. He liked to present his growing empire as an amiable partnership of east and west, though his high-minded internationalism was more a matter of low cunning. Alexander had inherited his father's diplomatic skills along with his ruthlessness, and he always preferred to be welcomed as a liberator to being loathed as an invader. So it was in Egypt. However cynical his actual motives may have been, his respectful posture was welcome to the Egyptians after the arrogant overlordship of Persia. When he founded his own new city, Alexandria, on Nile Delta, he was cementing the commercial links between Egypt and the Aegean.

King, pharaoh, god

The title of pharaoh could in any case hardly suffice for a man of Alexander's ambition. His work in Egypt done, he took time out from his campaign to

1

1. Cloak billowing and charger rearing, Alexander the Great strikes a suitably dramatic pose.

make an expedition of a more spiritual sort. Leaving his army behind him, he took a small party of attendants and set off southwestward through the desert.

Approximately a month later, he reached the Libyan oasis where the ram-horned god Ammon was reputed to live. An African god originally, Ammon had through several centuries of cultural interchange become associated with the Olympian Zeus. He was therefore an intriguing figure for Greek visitors to Africa. Alexander's motives in making the journey were very likely diplomatic to begin with – visiting local rulers who might assure the security of his borders with the west. What happened at Ammon, however, would be vital to his self-propagated myth. For it was the priests at the deity's shrine who first proclaimed Alexander's divinity, a status he insisted on from that time forward. Already amazed at his achievements, no one found it too hard to believe that the man who had gone into the desert should have come back an immortal god.

The road to Persepolis

His deity assured, Alexander set out for the Persian heartlands, marching his men northeastward across the Euphrates into Mesopotamia in the spring of 331. Darius prepared to meet him at Gaugamela, with – legend has it – no fewer than a quarter of a million men.

With six times as many troops as his would-be invader and 200 scythe chariots waiting to charge, Darius could hardly have imagined, for all his

▶ THE LIVING TANK

Alexander's army invading India faced a novel sort of weapon: trained elephants armoured up as living tanks (depicted on the bronze coin shown below). As the Macedonians went into action by the Hydaspes river, they found themselves confronting no fewer than 85 of these gigantic beasts, each bearing a castle-shaped cockpit from which archers directed a stinging rain of arrows. As so often before, however, Alexander's infantry simply held its nerve: even elephants could not push through the hedge of sarissa pikes. The elephants thus stalled, the infantry behind were pulled up in confusion. The Indians' secret weapon had only made matters worse.

earlier setbacks, that this was to be the Persian empire's last stand. But once again overwhelming odds became irrelevant in the face of the sheer discipline of Alexander's force. Arrows and javelins rained down on Darius's chariots, before the Macedonian ranks calmly parted to let them speed harmlessly through. Closing up again they thrust at the Persian centre which, now demoralized, broke and ran. Soon Alexander had captured Babylon, before going on to sack Persepolis, the seat of the Persian kings.

Even now Alexander was not satisfied. In 326 BC he crossed the mountains of the Hindu Kush: all India lay before him. An encounter on the banks of the Hydaspes river suggested that Indian armies were likely to fare no better against Alexander than Persian ones. But if he had nothing to fear from foreign forces, Alexander had finally to listen to his own. Though specialist mercenaries – archers, slingers and javelin-throwers – had been recruited in conquered territories along the way, the main force of Alexander's army had been with him when he left Macedonia. After eight years' campaigning they had finally had enough. Reluctantly, Alexander turned his face westward, and began retracing his steps. In the event, he got no further than Babylon, where at the age of 32 he was mysteriously taken ill and died.

There were rumours that Alexander had been poisoned by his lieutenants – a fit end for one who had himself quite possibly murdered his way to power. It is more likely, however, that the great conqueror died more prosaically, of natural causes – most probably malaria.

A DWINDLING EMPIRE

If Alexander's henchmen did not assassinate their commander, they soon revealed how vicious they could be in the pursuit of his power. For the next 40 years they fought for the succession, making a battleground of the empire he had built. In Egypt Alexander's friend Ptolemy took charge: he and his sons had some success in founding a dynasty. In the Middle East, after a long struggle, another of Alexander's officers, Seleucus, won the throne in a kingdom that included Syria, Mesopotamia and Persia. Greece and the Aegean fell to Antigonus and his heirs. It proved an uncomfortable inheritance: the Greek city-states found some of their old

1

independence now that the towering figures of Philip and Alexander had gone.

Like Alexander, his various successors proclaimed themselves gods. They emulated their mentor and model, too, by marrying local princesses as they conquered new territory, thus to some extent grafting themselves into the local power structures and buying the loyalty of their new-found subjects. The odds were ultimately against them, however. It had always been miraculous that one general and a single army should build and maintain an empire of this size. Their success in pulling off that miracle was testimony to Alexander's unique authority, and his skill in harnessing local pride and patriotism to his own imperial ends. Even as he conquered, he

2

1. Mask of the Greek god Zeus. The range of Zeus's authority was much extended by Alexander's victories, though adapted to fit in with local traditions.

2. From 400 BC onwards, Greek power, like Zeus's temple in Athens, would slowly fall into rack and ruin.

had persuaded people he was liberating them. His empire was to that extent a giant confidence trick, but it was a trick that worked. Alexander's authority had held even when he and his men had passed on and were carving out new territories thousands of miles away. It was inevitable that, with Alexander gone, his empire began imploding. The rivalries between his staff served only to bring forward that inevitability, though it remained, thanks to Alexander, a Greek or 'Hellenistic' world.

The Hellenistic age

Coming from 'Hellas', the name the Greeks gave their country, the word Hellenistic is, ironically, used only for this final period of Greek decline. Greece's time of true greatness had come and gone before Alexander made it an imperial power, but this did not lessen its influence in the world. Greek language and culture permeated much of western Asia in the age that followed – far more than when a strong Persia had kept Athenian influence at bay. While Greek generals besieged cities and laid waste to provinces in their apparently endless internecine struggles, the values of Greek civilization were more widely dispersed than ever. If some of the freshness of high Athenian classicism was gradually being lost, the interaction of Greek and Asian strands was enriching in itself.

The continuing importance of Greek civilization was, however, illusory in the sense that the best in 'Greek' culture no longer originated in Greece. What should have been the centre now seemed an increasingly irrelevant backwater in a world whose

 ## ATHENS ECLIPSED

Other Greek gods and goddesses may have looked with special favour on particular cities, but only Athena (depicted left, in a 5th-century BC marble statue) actually lent her name to a state. Myth had it that she sprang forth fully formed from the head of her father, the great god Zeus. Even in the illustrious company of the Olympian gods, she stood apart: as accomplished in weaving and the arts as she was fearsome in the field of war, she was both Athena Ergane (Athena the maker) and Athena Nike (Athena the bringer of victory). In the end, however, her association with Athens would prove limiting. As Athenian leadership began to flag, Athena in turn lost some of her lustre. Other Olympian deities, with less specific associations, were readily absorbed into the Roman pantheon. Much of the mythology surrounding Zeus gathered around Jupiter, the ruler of the Roman gods, while the Roman love goddess Venus is recognizably Aphrodite. The Roman goddess Diana inherited the chastity of the Greeks' virgin huntress Artemis, and the Romans' imperial Juno the haughtiness of Hera, Zeus's queen. But no place could be found for Athena, too closely identified with a single city whose own importance had long since passed.

1. His heroic life over, a Greek warrior falls, fatally wounded in the field.

centre of gravity had moved farther to the south and east. Alexandria now overshadowed Athens both as a merchant power and as a centre of culture; the old Greek colonies of Asia Minor had more economic energy than the mother cities on the mainland that first gave them birth. Farther west, an empire was arising that would one day make provinces of them all. At the end of the 6th century BC a small tribe in central Italy, the Latins, had shaken off the rule of their Etruscan masters. By the time the 3rd century BC began, all Italy was subject to Roman rule. Like the Greeks before them, the Romans founded coastal colonies, which brought them into conflict with the old Phoenician possession of Carthage on the coast of North Africa. That naval power at last destroyed, the Romans were effective rulers of the Mediterranean. As some of their legions spilled northward and

westward into Gaul, others shipped eastward across the Adriatic, to smash the Macedonian phalanx at Cynoscephalae. That defeat in 197 BC marked the end for ancient Greece as a sovereign state: Graecia had become a Roman province.

Not that Greek civilization was dead. Its influence could be traced in every aspect of the culture the Roman legions took with them across the ancient world from Syria to Scotland. Twenty-two centuries later the classical spirit lives on. Western politics and law, and institutions of society and state, would have been unthinkable without the example of the ancient Greek cities. Achievements in literature, art and architecture, and the aesthetic sense that orders our response: none of these can be conceived of without the precedents of classical culture. It is no exaggeration to say that, in ancient Greece, modernity was first imagined.

FURTHER INFORMATION

BOOKS

M.M. Austin and P. Vidal-Naquet (eds), *The Economic and Social History of Ancient Greece: An Introduction* (Batsford, London, 1977)
Documentary sources of the day provide vivid insights into the realities of life in ancient Greece.

Peter Beresford Ellis, *Celt and Greek: Celts in the Hellenic World* (Constable, London, 1997)
An illuminating account of a neglected aspect of Classical history.

John Boardman, *The Greeks Overseas: Their Early Colonies and Trade* (Thames & Hudson, London, 2nd edition, 1980)
Readable illustrated guide to Greece's colonial and cultural reach in the pre-classical world.

John Boardman, *The Oxford History of Classical Art* (Oxford University Press, 1993)
Illustrated survey of the artistic achievements of the classical Greeks and Romans.

Rodney Castleden, *Minoans: Life in Bronze-Age Crete* (Routledge, London, 1990)
Highly readable history of Minoan civilization.

John Chadwick, *The Mycenaean World* (Cambridge University Press, 1976)
A good general survey of a relatively little-known period.

Peter Green, *Alexander to Actium: The Hellenistic Age* (Thames & Hudson, London, 1990)
Authoritative history of the post-classical period.

Ian Morris, *Burial and Ancient Society: The Rise of the Greek City-State* (Cambridge University Press, 1987)
Provides insights into the earliest developments towards democracy.

Oswyn Murray, *Early Greece* (Fontana, London, 1980)
A narrative history of pre-classical Greece.

Colin Renfrew, *The Emergence of Civilization: The Cyclades and the Aegean in the Third Millennium BC* (Methuen, London, 1972)
Definitive account of what is known about the very earliest stages of Greek history.

Michael Woods, *In Search of the Trojan War* (BBC, London, 1985)
An enthralling introduction to a controversial subject, even if its conclusions are to some degree contentious.

R.E. Wycherley, *How the Greeks Built Cities: The Relationship of Architecture and Town Planning to Everyday Life in Ancient Greece* (W.W. Norton, New York, 1976)
An accessible approach to Greek history and culture through what is known about the towns and cities in which they lived.

INDEX